SOUTHEND-ON-SEA
A Pictorial History

SOUTHEND~ON~SEA
A Pictorial History

Jessie K. Payne

Phillimore

1985

Published by
PHILLIMORE & CO. LTD.
Shopwyke Hall, Chichester, Sussex, England

ISBN 0 85033 589 2

Printed and bound in Great Britain by
BIDDLES LTD.
Guildford, Surrey

LIST OF ILLUSTRATIONS

PREFACE AND ACKNOWLEDGEMENTS

This book is the realisation of a wish made a long time ago, which was to publish some of the many historic photographs of places and faces that were once well known in Southend. Some of the scenes recorded are no longer even a memory. Who would believe that a thatched cottage and a wood with a rookery once stood where Seaway now crosses York Road!

I hope that this pictorial history will give as much pleasure to its readers as it has given me in preparing it, and that it will help to preserve and make known a little more of Southend's long and often fasctinating history.

I particularly wish to thank the Essex Record Office and the County Archivist Mr. V. Gray, for permission to use photographs and the staff of the Southend branch for their unfailing help and courtesy; Southend Central Library for permission to use photographs from their collection in the Local Studies and Miss R. A. Stratton for her invaluable help; the Central Museum, Southend, for permission to use photographs and the Beecroft Art Gallery for permission to use no. 110; Mr. K. Crowe, keeper of Human History, Southend Central Museum, for kindly reading and making suggestions for most of the text; the *Evening Echo* for permission to use nos. 31, 35, 43, 67, 102, 106, 132, 134, 135, 145, 152, 157; Mr. E. M. Scratton for permission to use the photograph of Daniel Scratton; the churchwardens of All Saints' church, for permission to use no. 51; Essex Water Company for no. 96; Messrs. Marks & Spencer for nos. 137 and 138; Dr. T. Going for advice and help in making excellent photographic prints; Mr. J. D. Wood for photography; Mr. J. Kennedy Melling and Messrs. Percy Raven for help.

The picture of Caroline, Princess of Wales and Princess Charlotte is reproduced by gracious permission of Her Majesty, Queen Elizabeth II.

BIBLIOGRAPHY

Benton, P., *History of Rochford Hundred.*

Bride, H. N., *The Story of Southend Pier.*

Burrows, John W., *Southend Pier and its Story.*

Burrows, John W., *Southend-on-Sea and District*, 1970.

Burrows, V. E., *The Tramways of Southend.*

Deeping, Warwick (recollections), *St John's Parish Church, Southend-on-Sea.*

Dilley, Roy, *The Dream Palaces of Southend.*

Everritt, S., *Southend Seaside Holiday.*

Glennie, Donald (ed.), *Southend Review*, no. 1, 1949.

Goodale, A. P., *Holy Trinity, Southchurch, 1500 years of history.*

Goodale, A. P., *Southchurch, the History of a Parish.*

Hodgkins, John R., *The History of Cliff Town Congregational Church, 1799-1972.*

Kelly's *Directories of Essex.*

Listed Buildings, Town and Planning Act, 1947.

Dow, George, *London, Tilbury and Southend Album.*

Gowing, Ellis N., *Prittlewell Church*, 1932 and 1958.

Helliwell, Leonard, *The History of Prittlewell Priory*, 1970.

Helliwell, Leonard, *Southchurch Hall*, 1973.

Jennings, George, *Porters, Civic House and Mayor's Parlour*, 1938.

Melling, John K., *Southend Playhouses from 1793.*

Morant, P., *History of Essex.*

Nicholls, John F., *Southchurch Hall* (Museum handbook, 1936).

Pollitt, William, *Archaeology of Rochford Hundred and South-East Essex.*

Pollitt, William, *History of Prittlewell.*

Pollitt, William, *The Rise of Southend.*

Pollitt, William, *Some Literary Associations of Southend-on-Sea.*

Pollitt, William, *Southchurch and its Past.*

Pollitt, William, *Southend 1760-1860.*

Prittlewell Priory and Museum, History and Guide, 2nd edn.

Reaney, P., *Our Town, An encyclopedia of Southend-on-Sea and District* (Donald Glennie, *Place Names of Essex*).

Reynolds, *The Jesus Guild* (Museums leaflet no. 1).

Royal Commission on Historical Monuments, vol. IV (London 1923).

Salmon, *History of Essex*, 1740.

Shepherd, E. W., *The Story of Southend Pier.*

A Short History of St Mark's church, Cliff Town.

Smith, J. R., *Southend Past.*

Southend Standard.

Southend Waterworks Company, 1865-1965.

Waring, David, *A Hundred Years of All Saints', Southend-on-Sea.*

White's *Gazetteer and Directory of Essex*, 1863.

Wright, *History and Topography of Essex*, 1835.

The Area in Prehistoric, Roman and Saxon Times

The earliest evidence of human occupation in the area now covered by Southend is hand axes of the Palaeolithic Old Stone Age (200000-10000 B.C.), which were found at Roots Hall and other locations. These early men were hunter-gatherers who were dependent on hunting for their livelihood. When they had exhausted the supplies of game, nuts and berries in one area, they moved on to another where food was plentiful.

Prehistoric remains have been found in this area. In 1955 the remains of a late Neolithic burial (4000 to 2000 B.C.) was unearthed at the airport. This contained the skeleton of a girl of about fifteen years old. Workers in Thorpe Hall brickfield discovered the remains of an early Bronze Age (c.2000 B.C.) Beaker man in 1924. Buried with the skeleton were a flint dagger and a beaker, the type of pottery which gave its name to the people. Beaker men were farmers who came from the continent from an area between the Baltic and the Rhine. They introduced the use of bronze, cleared forests, built houses, wove cloth and made good pots.

During the whole of the Bronze Age, and for a long time afterwards, a lagoon covered a large part of what is now Southchurch. It extended from an inlet or inlets near the site of the North Sea Gas Offices on Eastern Esplanade to a point near Bournes Green. Bronze Age men camped on its shores, feeding on the shellfish and leaving behind them mounds of discarded shells as evidence.

Iron-using farmers came to Britain in about 550 B.C., heralding the Iron Age. In about 1926, 12 Iron-Age pots were found near the Prittle Brook and on Roots Hall Estate. The Romans also knew Southend. Urns have been found in Bournemouth Park Road and York Road, and a burial group was discovered in Prittlewell.

Saxons from north-east Europe entered the Thames from A.D. 350. They may have come up Porter's Creek, which at that time crossed the present York Road near Seaway and flowed almost up to Porters. It is thought that a Saxon village was in existence in Prittlewell in about A.D. 500 as in 1923 a Saxon cemetery was discovered to the east of Priory Park.

From about A.D. 850 the area was subject to attacks from the savage heathen Danes. They have left a small trace of their occupation of Southchurch in the name 'Thorpe', which means 'village'. The remains of a Danish invader who fell in battle more than a thousand years ago with an arrow embedded deep in his body were discovered at Shoebury in 1958.

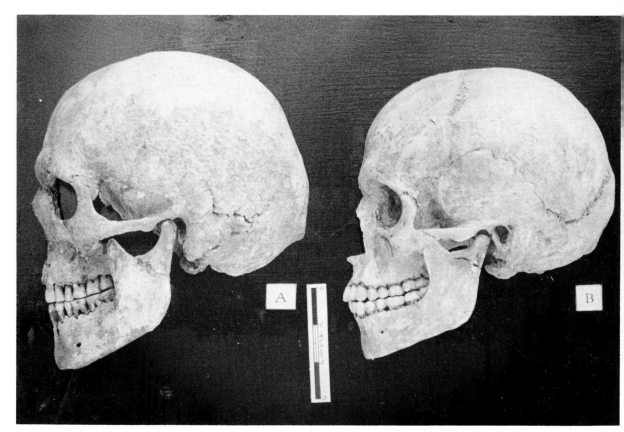

1. On the left is a skull of 'Beaker Man' (*c.*2000 B.C.), found at Thorpe Hall brickfield, 1924. On the right is a cast of a modern skull for comparison.

2. A collection of objects found in a Romano-British burial at Prittlewell, including urns, a glass bottle, a bronze flask, an iron lampholder and a bronze strigil or skin-cleansing scraper.

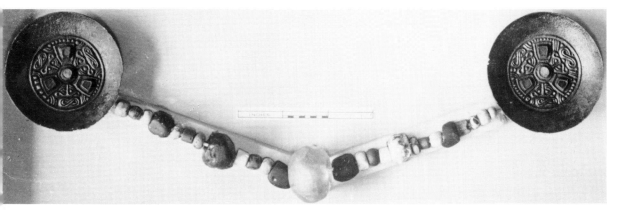

3. Gilt bronze brooches and beads, early seventh century in date, found in the Saxon cemetery east of Priory Park, Prittlewell.

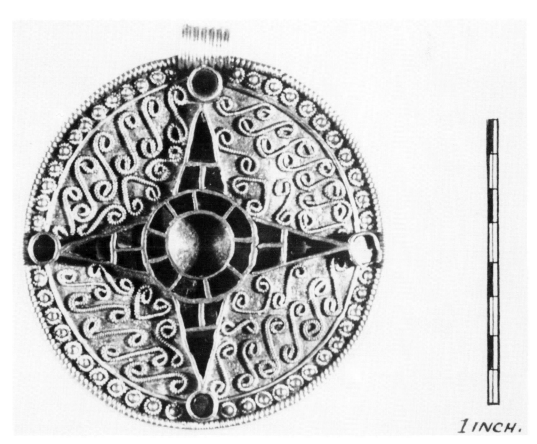

1 INCH.

4. A seventh-century Anglo-Saxon pendant set with a garnet, found in the same place.

5. The only remaining part of the Saxon church which stood on the site of the present chancel of St Mary's, Prittlewell, is this arch, first recognised for what it was in 1931.

6.   The present borough of Southend lies within the area which was listed under the manor of Prittlewell in Domesday Book, compiled for William the Conqueror in 1086. 'Swein holds Prittlewell in lordship for 7½ hides [a hide = approximately 120 acres]. Then [i.e. 1066] 7 villagers, now 4; then 14 smallholders, now 23. Then 2 ploughs (8 oxen per plough) in lordship, now 3. Then 7 men's ploughs, now 9. Pasture, 12 pigs; pasture, 200 sheep. Then 2 cobs, 8 cattle, 30 pigs, 100 sheep; now 1 cob, 3 foals, 13 cattle, 65 pigs, 200 sheep less 4, 66 goats, 9 beehives. Of this land, 1 free man holds 1 virgate which he could sell; but the jurisdiction lay in [the lands of] this manor. To [the lands of] this manor's church 2 men added 30 acres of another land. Value always £12. Of this manor, Grapinel holds ½ hide. 2 smallholders. 1 plough. Value 10s in the same assessment.'

Translation from *Domesday Book: Essex*, General editor John Morris, text and translation by Alexander Rumble (published by Phillimore & Co. Ltd., 1983).

The Manors

The manors were the homes of a number of important local families through the centuries. In the Domesday Survey of 1086, compiled for William the Conqueror to show the value of the land he had gained, Swein of Rayleigh Castle held Prittlewell, and Milton Hall and Southchurch Hall were held by Christchurch Priory, Canterbury.

In about 1100 Robert Fitzsweyn endowed the Cluniac Priory at Prittlewell and a large part of the area became monastic property. The priory did not, however, hold all of Prittlewell as the manor of Earls Hall with Polsted Wick was separate.

During the peasants' revolt, in 1381, rebels obtained and burnt the court rolls of Southchurch and Milton manors. These recorded the services and obligations which had to be rendered by the customary tenants.

After the dissolution of the monasteries, Prittlewell Priory and Milton Hall came into the hands of Sir Richard Riche. His name was appropriate as he became rich from the monastic properties given to him by the king. His heirs were the earls of Warwick, and from them the manors were purchased by the Scratton family. Daniel Scratton, who lived in the 19th century, was the last lord of the manor. Southchurch also belonged to Lord Riche and it later passed through the hands of a number of families. In 1650 the estate was divided into the Hall and Wick Farm.

There were originally two other manors in Southchurch parish. They were known as South Thorpe and North Thorpe. The name Thorpe is of Scandinavian origin; they were probably hamlets during the Danish supremacy. Thorpe Hall was held by Ingvar (a name of Danish origin) during the Confessor's reign, and is mentioned in Domesday Book. North and South Thorpe manors were united in the 15th century and no trace now remains of a manor house at North Thorpe. The 16th-century manor house of South Thorpe is now the Thorpe Hall Golf Club House.

7. Southchurch Hall (seen here about 1914) was the home of the de Southchurch family from about 1150 to 1350. By 1900, the present 14th-century building had become a farmhouse known as Whiffen's Farm. In 1925, members of the Dowsett family presented it to the Borough.

8. Southchurch Hall from the south before the restoration of 1929.

9. Southchurch Hall during restoration (1 October 1929), showing the porch probably added in the 16th century. The tracery is now preserved inside the Hall.

10. Manorial boundary plates in the seawall under the old gasworks, photographed on 8 May 1924. The inscriptions on them read: '1854. From these posts in a direct line to low water mark are the bounds of the manor sea grounds and fishery of Southchurch now belonging to George Asser White Welch Esquire' and on the other '1833. This post and others below denote the boundary of the manor of Prittlewell Priory and so continued with stones set in a straight line to low water'.

11. Nazareth House, formerly Milton Hall, about the turn of the century, before rebuilding. It came into the possession of the Sisters of Nazareth in 1880. In 1086 at the time of Domesday the manor of Milton was held by Christchurch, Canterbury. A large part of Milton was submerged by the sea during the period from the 14th to the 17th centuries. Until about 1740, it was said, the ruins of the church could be seen at low tide.

2. Chalkwell Hall, built in 1830, and seen here in 1905. The Hall and its Park were later purchased by the Corporation. The site was later developed for building. Two earlier houses had stood near the site previously.

3. Earls Hall, Prittlewell, which probably dated from the 17th century, was demolished in 1964. It is seen here in 1962. On the chimney stack was the coat of arms of the earls of Oxford who formerly held the manor, and it was sometimes called Earls Fee for this reason.

Farms

Most of the land in the area that now forms the Borough of Southend was originally farmland. Only two areas are still farmed; part of Temple Farm on the borough boundary, and part of Wick Farm, Southchurch, which is still farmed and has a new farmhouse in Wakering Road.

The other farms have disappeared without trace. Hamlet Farm, or Snells, was in Hamlet Court Road, and the 17th-century Hamstell farmhouse was in North Avenue. The origins of Hamstell Farm can be traced back to 1372 when it was known as Botelers Hampstall. Botelers referred to William Pincerna, the butler (1204). A brass portrait of Thomas de Staple, who held Hamstell Farm in 1372, can be seen in Sutton church. A field on this farm paid fine to the Whispering or Lawless Court, Rochford. The last tenant refused to comply with the old custom of giving to the landlord a fat goose at Michaelmas and a fat turkey at Christmas.

Until 1895 Woodgrange Drive was the chase leading from Southchurch Avenue to the door of Thames of Arnolds Farm. This was a long, rambling, white-plastered building originally called Facons or Fauns. It was said to be 400 years old and to have had a moat. It contained fine old panelling which was sold when it was destroyed.

Buttery's Farm, which stood at the end of the track leading from Southchurch Boulevard, was still being farmed in the 1950s. The old house was demolished at the beginning of the 1960s. It may have been the home of William de la Botery in 1395.

14. Thames or Arnolds' Farm, which stood in Woodgrange Drive, then the chase leading from Southchurch Avenue. This photograph dates from about 1880, and the house was demolished in 1895. It took its name from Mr. Arnold, first tenant and, after 1874, owner of the farm.

15. Wick Farm stood on Southchurch Boulevard, and had 14 rooms and a kitchen with a huge chimney stack. A stone slab was said to cover the entrance to an underground passage to the church. The farm had its own springs, one in the yard and one supplying the kitchen pump. A new farmhouse has been built in Wakering Road.

16. Daines Farm, Southchurch, although built around 1400, took its name from a farmer who occupied it in the 19th century. It originally stood near the junction of Shoebury Road and Southchurch Boulevard. It had previously been known as Bournes Green, Bawnes, Bornes or Bonours. This photograph was taken shortly before it was demolished in 1959.

17. Samuel's Farm, which stood on the Shoebury Road, Southchurch, dated from the 17th century, and was probably named after John Samuel who held it in 1270. It was demolished in 1963.

18. Green Shutters Farm, seen here about 1900, formerly called Berlands or Barlings, stood nearly opposite the *Ploug* at Westcliff. In 1469 John Quyke of Berlonds bequeathed some land in North Shoebury to the Jesus Guild of Prittlewe

19. Colemans Farm probably took its name from John Coleman, who owned the farm in 1304, although the building seen here (in 1963) dated from the 17th century. It stood near the General Hospital which is built on part of its land, and was demolished in 1970.

20. Temple Farm was built during the 16th century, but the name was applied to a building on the site as early as 1220. It belonged first to the Order of Knights Templars and later to the Knights Hospitallers. On the dissolution of the latter order in 1543 it became the property of Lord Riche. The last person to be hanged for sheep-stealing came from this farm.

The Priory

In about 1110 Robert Fitzsweyn endowed the Cluniac priory of Prittlewell. It was a dependent house of the priory of St Pancras at Lewes. The church was much larger than that of Prittlewell and the priory was probably the most wealthy in Essex. There were never more than 18 monks at the priory. They wore a black frock or cassock, white woollen tunic and black scapulary.

Cluniacs followed the rule of St Benedict as interpreted by Berno, who founded the Cluniac order at Cluny in France in 912. The foundation of the order was to fulfil a desire to follow more closely the rule of St Benedict, with certain adaptations.

As the Cluniacs were dependent on the head house, and the head of Cluny appointed the priors of all their houses, this made Prittlewell an alien order. When England was at war with France alien houses were taken into the king's hands. Prittlewell became free of foreign allegiance in 1374 when Edward III declared the mother house of Lewes and its dependent houses to be denizen.

The monks would have been a familiar sight in the surrounding countryside. They served the churches of North Shoebury, Eastwood and Prittlewell and held property around Prittlewell and further afield in Essex.

Much gossip must have resulted from the fight in the priory church in 1321. A long-drawn-out argument had been raging over who should be prior. Eventually it reached such proportions that Prior William de Auvergnat was attacked and wounded in the head while celebrating mass at the high altar.

No doubt the poor of Prittlewell missed the distribution of alms from the priory when it was suppressed in 1536. It was purchased by Thomas Audley on payment of £400 to the king.

21. (*opposite*) Prittlewell Priory as it would have looked in the 14th century, from the east.

22. (*above*) Prittlewell Priory about 1872. Until 1869 it was the home of Daniel Scratton, master of the South Essex Hunt. He kennelled the hounds at the Priory.

23. (*below*) The Prior's Chamber, Prittlewell Priory. Its roof dates from about 1323. Known also as the Great Chamber, in monastic days it had green hangings, a bed with a feather mattress and a tapestry cover, a table, half a dozen stools, a chair and a branched latten candlestick.

The Rise of Southend

'Southend' was originally the south end of the lane leading from Prittlewell to the south. There is mention in 1309 of corn being carried to 'Strathende' to be loaded on to boats for transport to London, and it is thought that it was probably near the site of the Kursaal. It was not until the end of the 15th century that the name 'Southend' is mentioned. A will of 1481 mentions a lane called Southend in the parish of St Mary's, Prittlewell. It probably led to a few fishermen's huts and a jetty.

At the time of the dissolution of the monasteries a tenement and 10 acres of land in 'Southende' were in the possession of Thomas Larkyn. The first permanent dwellings were probably those of oyster fishermen.

In the second half of the 18th century the *Ship* inn was built to accommodate a growing number of visitors, and by 1787 a regular stage coach plied between the *Ship* in Southend and the *Bull* in Aldgate. In 1793 a theatre was opened and in 1795 the Caroline cold and warm sea water baths were opened. These were named after Princess Caroline of Brunswick who had married the Prince of Wales that year. Southend then occupied the area around the Kursaal site. Southend Lane was the principal road into it. It consisted of what is now Old Southend Road, part of York Road and the southern end of Southchurch Avenue.

In 1791 Thomas Holland began to build the Grand Terrace, Hotel and Library on the cliffs to the west of the old town. This was known as New Southend, or the upper town. When, in 1804, Princess Caroline visited Southend the Terrace, Hotel and Library were given the title Royal. By 1806 Southend had become a resort of note, patronised by the aristocracy and the fashionable world. However, those who arrived by water had to suffer the indignity of being carried ashore on the backs of fishermen. In 1828 it was decided that an increase in trade and traffic would be assured if a pier was erected, and at a meeting at the *Royal* Hotel the decision was taken to build one. The first site to be proposed was near the Kursaal site and the first section of the pier was opened in 1830. It was extended in 1846 and eventually became the longest pier in Europe.

When the railway reached the town in 1856, Southend was no longer 'an asylum to the lovers of quiet' and the cultured type of visitor. The population grew fast, and housing estates sprang up. The first to be built was the Cliff Town Estate, followed by Porters town near Porters, and the Park Estate. The High Street developed from a country lane into a shopping area.

In 1889 the Great Eastern Railway was extended and a station was built at the end of Victoria Avenue. The town grew quickly and achieved municipal status in 1892. In 1914 Southend became a county borough.

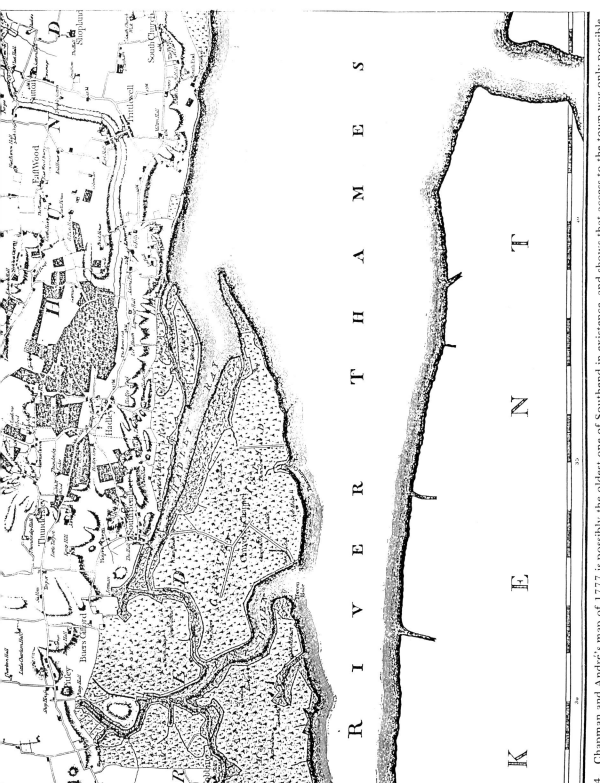

24. Chapman and André's map of 1777 is possibly the oldest one of Southend in existence, and shows that access to the town was only possible through Sutton Road and a lane by Thames Farm, following the line of Old Southend Road, and reaching the shore by the Kursaal site. An area of common land is shown extending along what is now Eastern Esplanade.

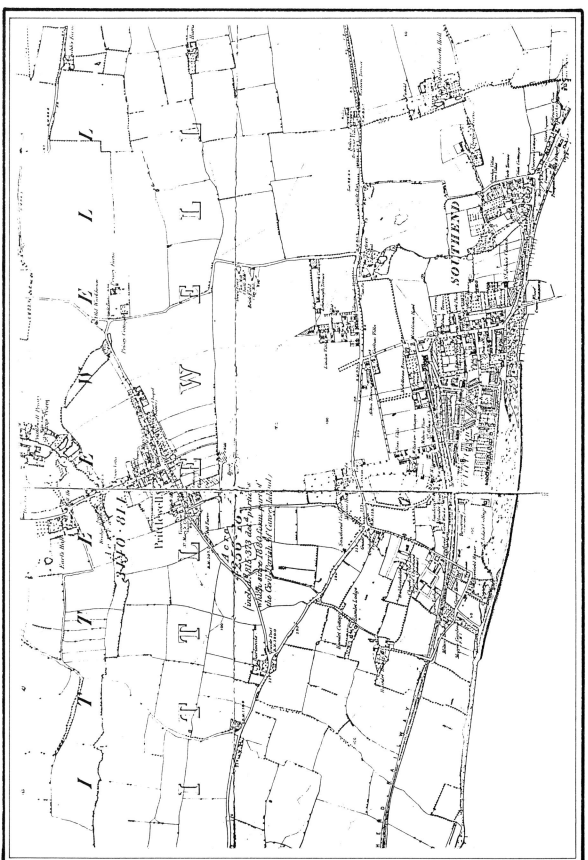

25. On this Ordnance Survey map of Southend (1873), we can see that the London, Tilbury and Southend Railway then terminated at the High Street and Victoria Avenue, as only partly built. The author's grandmother remembered walking through fields from Prittlewell to Southend

26. Mr. Ingram built his warm baths in 1804 on a site below the *Royal Hotel*, the outline of which can be seen through the trees. By 1841 they were owned by Thomas Ingram, who is shown with his family in this view of 1865. The pony was employed to pump water from an artesian well. The baths were demolished in 1879.

27. Marine Parade, about 1870. Note the wide green between the seashore and the road.

28.   Marine Parade, about 1875. The Ivy House is on the extreme right and Dowsett's shop in the centre.

29.   Marine Parade and the *Falcon* public house, about 1880. The *Falcon* was originally a private house, no. 4 Strutt's Parade, named after John **James** Strutt, second Baron Raleigh, who built it.

30. The *Hole in the Wall* and the first Southend bank on Marine Parade, 1878. The former became the *Borough Arms* and is now the *Liberty Belle*. The bank was probably a branch of Sparrow Tufnell and Co. of Chelmsford.

31.   The pier entrance as it appeared in 1880. The board at the entrance gives pier dués as the Corporation landing jetty was not in existence. The concert hall, which stood approximately on the site of the Pier Pavilion, had a tent awning as a roof; when the horse-drawn trams wanted to come through during a performance, the awning was drawn back and the audience moved their seats to allow the trams to pass.

32.   The pier and Pier Hill about 1869.

Pier Trams, Southend-on-Sea (1870).

33. Horse-drawn trams on the pier, 1870.

34. The inaugural run of the first electric tram to be used on the pier, 1889—claimed to be also the first in England.

35.   The beach near Prospect Place, *c.* 1900. Prospect Place was demolished in the mid-1950s.

36.   These young girls are enjoying a donkey ride on Darlow's Green in 1906. Behind them are the Methodist Free Chapel and the *Castle Hotel*, then situated on the sea side of Marine Parade. The Sharp family were donkey-owners in Southend for many generations.

37. Westcliff Esplanade under construction, 1904.

38. Eastern Esplanade under construction, 1907.

CENTRAL BEACH, SOUTHEND ON SEA.

39. Central Beach, Southend, about 1905. In the background can be seen Absolom's two floating baths, one for ladies and children, and one for gentlemen. They could be used only when the tide was out, and were discontinued after the First World War.

40. The bathing machines on the beach west of the pier were for ladies and children only: men had their own machines elsewhere.

41.   The crowded beach near the Kursaal in pre-First World War days. Note the sailing barges, a common sight at the time.

42. The pierhead extension, summer 1907. The ladies are carefully keeping the sun off their faces—sunbathing had not yet become fashionable.

43. A view of the pier and the statue of Queen Victoria that stood on Pier Hill at the beginning of this century. It now stands on the cliffs.

44. In November 1908 the pier was damaged by the Thames Conservancy hulk *Marlborough* which broke loose from her moorings in a gale. Sixty feet of decking were destroyed.

Royal Southend

In 1801 a little girl could be seen sitting on Southend beach, busily making necklaces from the hard black berries of seaweed. This was no ordinary little girl; she was the five-year-old Princess Charlotte of Wales, who had been sent there by her physicians for the seabathing. She was staying at Southchurch Lawn (now Eton House School) and she patronised Mrs. Glasscock's bathing machines by the *Hope* and *Ship* hotels. On Sundays she attended Southchurch parish church and heard the Rev. Archer, the hunting parson, preach.

Two years later her mother, Princess Caroline of Brunswick, the unfortunate wife of the Prince Regent, paid a three-month visit to Southend. She occupied three houses in Royal Terrace and thereby gave it the title 'Royal'. She too bathed at Glasscock's machines. In 1806 there was an enquiry into the conduct of the princess. It was alleged by a man named Robert Bidgood that a Captain Manby, whose ship was lying off Southend, had visited the Terrace and that he had slept in the Princess's room. Bidgood's allegation stated that a basin and towels were found where he thought they should not have been placed. However, two maid servants denied this and the allegation was not proved.

Some seventy years later Southend had another royal visitor, Princess Louise, Duchess of Argyll, the fourth daughter of Queen Victoria. Her husband, who was a voluntary officer, was on a course of gunnery instruction at Shoeburyness. The princess and her husband stayed at The Lodge, in the High Street.

45. Royal Terrace, 1872.

46. Caroline, Princess of Wales and Princess Charlotte, 1802, from the painting by Sir Thomas Lawrence in the Royal Collection, Buckingham Palace. (*Reproduced by courtesy of Her Majesty Queen Elizabeth II.*)

47. Royal Terrace and the *Royal Hotel* were built between 1791 and 1793. They are seen here in about 1880.

48. This timber house, which still stands although partly hidden by the General Post Office in Weston Road, was formerly known as The Lodge. It was the home of the Reverend Fletcher, minister of Cliff Town Church (1830-42) and Princess Louise stayed here in 1873.

Churches

St Mary's church, Prittlewell, has a history that goes back to the early seventh century. It is one of the few Essex churches mentioned in the Domesday Survey of 1086. It was enlarged during the Norman period, and in the 15th century it was altered again and the fine tower added, built of stone from Kent. The south aisle was the chapel of the Jesus Guild *c*.1478-1548, a local socio-religious guild. Before 1842 St Mary's was the parish church of Southend, but in that year Southend was made an ecclesiastical parish.

The small church of Southchurch was enlarged in 1906 and again in 1932. It was first built between 1120 and 1150, but there has probably been a church on that site since 824.

The rapid expansion of the town led to the necessity for more churches, and in 1877 a new ecclesiastical district was formed. This supplied the needs of Porters Town, a housing estate that had been built near Porters. Miss E. A. Heygate gave the site on which All Saints' church, Queensway, was built, and the present church was completed in 1888.

St Mark's church in St John's Road belonged to the Baptist Church. In 1882 a new Baptist church building, which cost £950, was dedicated. Charles Spurgeon preached at the opening services. This building became too small for the congregation and the site of the present Avenue Baptist church was purchased and the old building sold to St John's to become St Mark's.

In 1892 £198 was paid for a Mission Room at Westcliff, and on 30 March that year the building opened. Six years later, on 17 June 1898, the foundation stone of St Alban the Martyr was laid by Bishop Festing of St Albans.

William Gregson, a Southend solicitor, gave some land in York Road for St Erkenwald's church. A temporary iron church was erected in 1903, but this was said to be so overcrowded that it became very necessary to build a large church. A committee advertised that a competition was to be held. The competitors were asked to design the new church, parish hall and clergy house. Sir W. J. Tapper's design was selected, and the foundation stone was laid in 1905.

The Methodists began to hold open-air services near the *Army and Navy* public house (renamed Stocks) in 1850, and a house in East Street, Prittlewell was the first meeting-place of the Baptists in 1823. There were very few Roman Catholic families in Southend during the last century, and the oldest Catholic church is Our Lady Help of Christians and St Helen, completed in 1903.

49. St Mary the Virgin, Prittlewell, 1869. About this time there were complaints that dogs and cattle grazing in the churchyard were uncovering bones and skulls. On the south side of the tower can be seen the school kept by the Jesus Guild in the 16th century, which was entered by the door seen at the west end of the south aisle.

50. The church of Southchurch is seen here from the north, c.1869. It was enlarged in 1906 and again in 1932, and the Norman arch and windows shown here were removed to the present nave and chancel. Note the rough state of the road.

51.   The west front of St John the Baptist church, Southend, in 1879.
In 1832 it had been decided to build a chapel of ease because of the
growing population of Southend, and its distance from the existing
parish church. The church was built in 1840 at a cost of £1,500.

52.   The first church on the site of All Saints', Queensway. The galvanised iron building (the 'Tin Church')
seated 500 persons and cost £5,500. It was dedicated by the bishop of St Albans on 27 July 1877, and the
preacher was the Reverend Henry White, Chaplain of the Savoy and Chaplain in Ordinary to the Queen.

53. St Alban's church, Westcliff, c.1902. The
chancel, tower and transepts were completed
and consecrated in 1904.

54. St Erkenwald's church, 1910, soon after
the completion of the nave and baptistry, the
building of which had formed the second phase
of construction. The original 'Tin Church' can
be seen on the right. The church was declared
redundant in 1977.

55. Cliff Town church, 1869. The first church was at the junction of Clarence Street and High Street. The foundation stone of the present church was laid on 30 May 1865 by Isaac Perry, a partner of Frederick Wells, Brewers of Chelmsford. Five months later the new building was opened. It was designed by W. Allen Dixon of Kentish Town, London.

56. The Methodist chapel on Marine Parade, c.1900. It housed the so-called 'Free Methodists' who had broken away from the old Wesleyan Conference, and its foundation stone was laid on 12 June 1866. Michael Tomlin, a Leigh fisherman who started services in a coal warehouse in Southend, also preached here.

Homes

The oldest house in the area which is still standing is Southchurch Hall, which was built in the 13th century. Porters probably dates from the 15th century, the houses opposite Prittlewell church were built in the 16th century and No. 30 East Street, Prittlewell, is a very good example of an 18th-century building.

Royal Terrace is the most notable of the buildings that represent Old Southend. On Pier Hill are two old houses with canopied round bay upper windows. One was the home of Lady Denys in the 19th century. They are now occupied by amusement arcades. A little wooden house and shop hides behind a modern front on Marine Parade. In the 1950s it was owned by Murrel's who still sold shellfish there. The business had been in existence since 1838.

General Goodday Strutt would be very surprised if he could see the part of his home that survives above Las Vegas on Marine Parade. The house was known as Rayleigh House and was built in 1800 by Lord Rayleigh. The pavement in front of the Falcon was called Strutt's Parade. The general used to sit in his bay window to watch the shipping and, with Lady Denys, objected very strongly when it was suggested that the site of the pier might be opposite his house.

There were many little thatch-roofed cottage in the area during the last century. One such stood near Westcliff High School until 1954 when it was destroyed by fire as it was in the path of the second carriageway of Eastwood Lane.

57. The Mayor's Parlour, Porters, in 1910. The name of the house appears to derive from the Porter family: Lawrence le Porter held land in Prittlewell in 1305. The house dates from the late 15th or early 16th centuries and has panelling containing early 16th-century carved figures. There is a secret hiding place, and a tradition of a hidden passageway to the sea. Benjamin Disraeli stayed here in 1833/4.

58.   Reynolds, West Street, Prittlewell, seen here in about 1896, stood on a site now occupied by the Southend Amateur Boxing Club and the *Blue Boar* extension. It was built in the 14th century, and its name may derive from Robert Reynolds, accused of murdering his wife in 1388. The man on the left with the bowler hat is William Wallis, grocer and post master from about 1868-98.

59.   Rear view of Reynolds, in 1890, showing the elaborate 17th-century pargetting. The house was demolished in 1906 for the construction of an extension to the *Blue Boar*.

60. The fireplace at Reynolds, dating from about 1450, exposed during demolition in 1906. It is now on display in Southend Central Museum and features the monogram 'I.H.S.' between supporting trees, symbolising Christ crucified between thieves.

61. (*opposite above*) Bridge House was built about 1747, stood opposite Priory Park and was an appendage to a tanyard. In the latter half of the 19th century it belonged to the Drapers' Company. This photograph was taken in 1965.

62. (*opposite below*) Roots Hall, which stood on the north side of West Street, Prittlewell, was probably of 18th-century date, but had an older cellar. It is seen here in 1899. In 1511 it had been known as 'Rowards' but the name was corrupted to Roots Hall. The name survives as Southend United Club Stadium is on the site of its grounds.

63. (*above*) Camper House stood on Eastern Esplanade, Southend, and this photograph was taken about 1880-1890. A lady has informed the author that her grandmother lived here as a bride in the last century, and reared a family of 19 children. The name survives in 'Camper Road', and originated from an 18th-century Prittlewell family.

64.   Cottages nos. 48 to 58 East Street, Prittlewell, in 1926. When they were built Southend was little more than a straggling line of cottages along the line of the present Marine Parade and Eastern Esplanade. No. 52 was the home of Mr. John Perry, as it had sheltered his father and grandfather before him. Mr. Perry could remember the old Prittlewell Fair.

65.   The junction of East Street and North Street (now Victoria Avenue) in 1926. The house at the extreme corner was once the butcher's shop of John Dowsett. Next door on the north side were some premises which were at one time occupied by Mr. H. Garon, founder of Messrs. H. Garon Ltd. All these buildings except the brick house on the right were demolished in 1935.

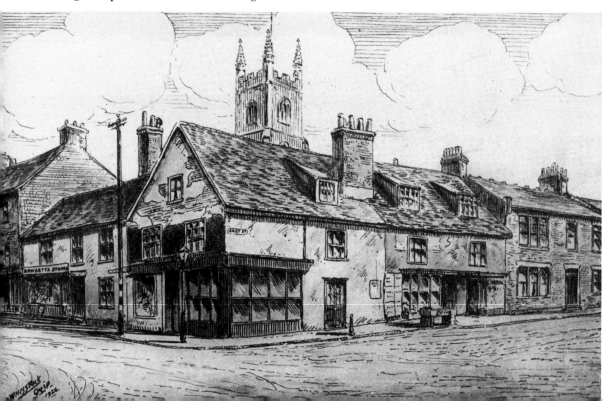

66. Deeds Cottages and the Old Bakery, on the north corner of West Street, in 1945. All these properties were built in the 16th century, and Deeds Cottages were demolished in the 1950s.

67. Albert Square, which stood behind shops near the Kursaal on Marine Parade. These small wooden cottages were built of old ships' timbers, some washed up on the beach. There was only one narrow entrance passage to the square. It was possible once to feed the cows on Arnolds' Farm from the windows on the north side, but the farm is now covered by the Kursaal and the new housing estate.

68. Grovefields, Heygate Avenue, *c.*1925. It was formerly the old vicarage for St. John's church.

69. The old rectory, West Street, Prittlewell. Built in 1865, it cost £3,800 to erect, the cost including the sinking of a well. The previous rectory was a small wooden house standing on the site which is now occupied by the school in East Street.

70. The Oaks, Southchurch Road, before demolition in 1958. It took its name from two trees that once stood in the front garden. In 1777, however, it was known as Tile House. Many years ago the body of an unknown woman was found here after it had been left empty for a long time, and old residents claimed to have seen her ghost. A garage now stands on its site near Brighton Avenue.

71. The Glen, Southchurch, stood on the corner of Southchurch Avenue and Southchurch Road, and was built in a quarry. In the First World War both British and Belgian wounded were nursed here by the Red Cross. It was demolished in the 1960s.

72. An old Dutch cottage which stood in Thorpe Hall Avenue before the land was sold for building.

73. The Bog House, a thatched cottage that stood in York Road, probably near Seaway, a century or so ago. It owed its name to the marshy nature of its site. Behind the cottage was a rookery. The picture is taken from a painting.

74. The Shepherd's Cottage on the west corner of Hamlet Court Road,
*c.*1912. It was so called because it was built on manorial waste ground by
Robert Scratton, and was occupied by his shepherd, John Dowsett, from
1874 until his death in 1881, and then by Dowsett's wife Mary until 1912.

75. In the last century these building stood on the corner where the entrance to the Kursaal now is.

76. This thatched cottage stood on the corner of Milton Road and London Road, opposite the *Cricketers*.

77. Old cottages in Southchurch Road, 26 January 1914. The Southend Town Council bought the land on which they stood, and which formerly belonged to Southchurch Hall, for development. On the site of the cottage at the right of the picture the public baths (now offices) were built. Lifstan Way now runs by the side of this spot.

78. Pleasant Row, Pleasant Road, built in 1767 by John Remnant, 'with good accommodation and fireing' for the oyster fishermen. The cottages were demolished in the 1960s.

Inns and Alehouses

Southend now has only two old inn buildings, the *Minerva* and the *Britannia* on the sea front. Prittlewell had four inns in 1769; of these only the *Blue Boar* and the *Spread Eagle* remain. The *Cricketers* in London Road was once two cottages and opened as an inn in 1866.

On the north-east corner of Prittlewell churchyard the *King's Head* once stood. It has been suggested that this and other property came in existence in the Middle Ages when some semi-permanent structures were erected adjacent to the churchyard for the performance of mystery plays, or for use during annual fairs, and during the course of the years these became permanent buildings. At the end of the 18th century a ball was held at the *King's Head* and a party from Southchurch Wick Farm travelled to the inn in a bathing machine. The *King's Head* also supplied beer for the bell ringers.

The *Spread Eagle* at Prittlewell was once connected with the cruel sport of cock fighting. In the *Chelmsford Chronicle* of 2 March 1787 it was stated that a main of cocks was to be fought on the 7th of the month at the *Spread Eagle* in Prittlewell between 'the gentlemen of that place and the gentlemen of Great Wakering'. The *Spread Eagle* was reconstructed in 1923. The only reminder of its past is its coaching yard where the Southend-Cambridge coach picked up passengers.

79. The *Hope*, Marine Parade, in 1905. The building dates from the late 18th century. There used to be a stone in Prittlewell churchyard to John Capon of the *Hope Inn*, Southend, who died on 10 October 1797. The manor court for Milton Hall used to be held here. A doctor who visited it in 1841 spoke of 'an exceedingly civil and comely landlady with pretty daughters all anxious to please'.

80. The *Royal Hotel* in 1874. An advertisement for the hotel early last
century stated that K. Miller was 'replete with gratitude for the many
favours conferred upon him by the nobility and gentry . . . and respectfully
informs them that the hotel had an elegant assembly room and coffee room
wherein are regularly taken the daily papers' as well as wines of the best
vintage and excellent stabling.

81. The old Ivy House on Marine Parade in 1850. No drinks could be obtained there then. An old inhabitant
remembered getting birds' eggs from the ivy, and also that the water supply came from the Kursaal area.

82. The *Britannia* public house near the Kursaal, Eastern Esplanade, about 1890.

83. The 18th-century *Ship Inn*, Marine Parade, in 1860. It was said to have connections with smuggling, and in 1797 it was the headquarters for the leaders of the Nore mutiny. By 1824 it was the principal hotel of the lower town, and in 1832 boasted hot and cold baths. Note the green before the house. It was rebuilt in 1955.

84. The original *Castle Hotel*, which stood just to the east of the Kursaal, on the opposite side of the road. It marked the limits of the Old Town, and beyond it were fields.

85.   The *Minerva*, Eastern Esplanade, about 1890. It was formerly the Great House built on the wasteland of Prittlewell Manor by Abraham Vandervord in 1793, and was named after its owner's barge. The manorial court of the Priory manor was held here at one time.

86.   The *Halfway House*, seen here in 1906, was built on Southchurch Beach, now Eastern Esplanade, in 1870. It was so called because it was halfway between Southend and Shoebury. Note that at the time the photograph was taken there was no seawall and the road was still unmade. The pub was used for coroners' inquests on drowned persons in the 19th century.

87. In 1682 the *White Horse* was one of the few dwellings in Southchurch and was surrounded by fields. It is seen here in 1890. In 1701 the innkeeper, John Dursley, was also the parish constable.

88. The *Fox and Hounds*, a beerhouse in East Street, which supplied beer for the bellringers. It was kept by **Jo**seph Garrard from *c.*1874 to *c.*1890. This photograph dates from about 1890.

Education

It is probable that the education of suitable pupils was originally undertaken by the monks of Prittlewell priory and according to records, a school was maintained by the Jesus Guild attached to St Mary's church. It is likely that this school was continued after the suppression of the guild for there is a reference to a schoolmaster in 1581, and in 1627 a scholar was sent from Prittlewell to Sidney Sussex College, Cambridge.

In 1727 the lord of the manor, Daniel Scratton, and the Rev. Thomas Case, the vicar, gave a building near to the south of the bridge at Prittlewell, on the east side of the road, with certain lands. This was to provide a school for 10 poor children and for a qualified schoolmaster to teach reading, writing, and the catechism and principles of the Christian religion according to the usage of the Church of England. In 1739 Scratton improved the endowment to provide education for 16 poor boys.

The school was enlarged in 1817 to accommodate more children and to include girls. In 1836 the minimum age for admission was seven years. All children except the 16 boys admitted under the 1739 endowment paid one penny a week. There were about 80 children in the school then.

In 1890 Southend had the London Road Board Schools which were erected in 1880 for 700 children, and the National Mixed School which was erected in 1860. For those who could afford to pay for their children's education there was a choice of schools and a college in Southend. Several of the five schools for girls were kept by sisters who were unlikely to have been qualified. Two schools did not specify whether they catered for girls or boys, which probably meant that they were infant schools. There was a boarding school at Grove House.

Ann Arnold started a Dame School at Southchurch in 1849 in a house opposite the church. She also ran a shop. Later this old house became the village post office. It was demolished when the boulevard was constructed in 1913.

A National School was established in Southchurch by trust deed dated 19 Feburary 1857. It was enlarged in 1898 but it was closed down in December 1948 because it failed to meet the requirements of modern education. The log books of this school illustrated the great changes in education and child life. Holidays were given for children to go rook scaring, and many absences were recorded for pea picking and the harvest.

89. St John's College on the Cliffs, 1872. St John's Court flats are on this site today.

90. (*left*) The former Prittlewell schoolhouse, 1954. Formerly known as Glynds, and built in the 17th century, it first became a schoolhouse in 1727 with an endowment by Daniel Scratton to allow 10 boys to have free education 'according to the usage of the church of England'. It was demolished later in the 1950s.

91. (*below*) St John's National School, 4 February 1910. It stood near the *Castle Inn* in Lower Southend, and was erected by subscription in 1855. It was controlled by trustees—the vicar of St John's, the churchwardens and the lord of the manor.

92.   Bournemouth Park Junior School in 1908, with the open fields behind. It had been built in the previous year.

93.   Lord Avebury laying the foundations of the Technical School, Victoria Circus, 1901.

94. The Countess of Warwick opening the Technical School in 1902. (Photograph by Lord Avebury.)

95. Empire Day celebrations at the Technical College, June 1905.

Water Supply and Sanitation

Up to the last century Southend and the surrounding parishes had to rely on wells, the Prittle Brook and even ponds for their water. Contamination of these supplies occurred very easily and in 1800 there was a serious outbreak of typhoid in Prittlewell in which 10 people died. Southend already had a main water supply but Prittlewell people were reluctant to change to such a new-fangled idea. The water company sent pure water in water carts during the epidemic, and mains were later laid in the village.

In 1856 the waterworks was built by the firm of Thomas Brassey, the great railway builder. He built the railway from London to Southend, and then built the waterworks to supply his steam engines. At first there was only one reservoir which was in Milton Road. Until 1871 the waterworks was a private undertaking, after which it became a limited company.

In Southend the Cliff Town Estate was put onto main drainage in 1866, but the rest of the town had no sewage system save that the refuse was carried by pipes to the foreshore and there discharged by numerous outfalls. Apart from the very serious outbreak of typhoid in 1800, there was another in 1879 and again in 1891.

96. The pumping station in Milton Road, 1879.

97. The pump at Prittlewell was erected by the parish in 1814. The original one was removed when the bridge over the Prittle Brook was rebuilt in 1800. Part of the pump (seen here *c.*1890) still stands near the entrance to Prittlewell Priory.

Transport

By 1821 visitors were able to travel to Southend by the *Rival*, the *Dispatch* and the *Wonder* coaches. Some visitors came by sea but the passage was slow, uncomfortable and sometimes dangerous and landing was difficult. Passengers came ashore in small dinghies and were carried from these on the backs of fishermen. The advent of the steam boat in 1819 made the journey quicker, cheaper and easier but the difficulty in landing still had to be resolved. The new pier, which was built in 1830, was not taken to deep water and could not be used as a landing place at low tide. Passengers had to be transferred to a vessel stationed permanently in deep water and then taken in boats to the pier head. A structure called 'the Lighthouse' or 'the Mount' was later built in deep water, from which which boats took passengers to the pier head or at low tide to a causeway. In 1846 the pier was extended to deep water.

In 1854 the railway was completed in Southend. It was originally planned to run along the foreshore from Leigh to the pier. There was to be access from the Shrubbery to the beach by a level crossing and a footbridge. No locomotive was to blow off steam within half a mile of the Royal Terrace. The residents of the Terrace strongly objected to the railway and the plan was altered to bring it along its present route.

The first mechanical transport to replace horses in the town were the electric Corporation trams. The tramway system was formally opened on 18 July 1901. This was followed in 1906 by permission from the town council (by a narrow majority) to the Southend and District Motor Omnibus Co. to run a bus service. A proviso was made that there was a maximum speed of eight miles per hour and in the High Street this was lowered to six miles per hour.

98. Sharp's donkey chaise, one of the earliest conveyances in Southend for visitors. This photograph is reproduced from a painting of 1844.

99. The London, Tilbury and Southend Railway opened in March 1856. Fares were 3s 6d (17½p) for a first-class single, 2s 6d (12½p) for a second-class single, and the journey took 95 minutes. This photograph shows the railway station at Southend in 1879.

100. The Corporation Tram Offices, Victoria Circus, on 23 May 1910. The houses behind the offices were later the site of shops and the Talza Arcade, and the spot is now occupied by the Hammerston development.

101. This tram outside All Saints' church in 1924 was about to go on a circular tour through Southchurch Boulevard and Thorpe Hall Avenue to Eastern Esplanade. The shops in the background were demolished when the roundabout was built.

02. A tram on the Southchurch Boulevard.

03. A charabanc full of visitors parked outside the *Railway Hotel*, Cliff Town Road, about 1905. At the back of the coach a lady is wearing one of the 'motor veils' used to secure the large hats which were then fashionable.

104. On 5 December 1914 this bus was travelling along Station Road in Westcliff when a gust of wind caught the driver's cap. He temporarily lost control and the bus ran onto the railway embankment, through a hedge and turned over. The passengers were shaken but unhurt.

Industry

The main industry in the area was originally agriculture and many sheep were kept on the marshes. An account roll of Southchurch manor for 1364 shows that there were 252 sheep at Southchurch and 394 on Canvey Island. The sale of wool yielded £10 5s. 5d. Milk from the ewes which, mixed with cow's milk, was made into hard cheese which had good keeping qualities and was eaten by the labouring classes at the that time, realised £2 2s. 6d.

The Domesday Survey of 1086 records that there were two fisheries at Southchurch. In 1381 the lord of the manor of Southchurch granted three men license to fish upon the Southchurch sands 'without the place of the keddles'. Keddles were probably long nets hung on stakes and arranged in the form of a letter V, the point of which was on the seaward side, the open end towards the shore. Fish were carried in by the tide and became trapped in the net when the tide receded. Keddles still existed as late as 1772.

In about 1700 a fisherman named Outing discovered by accident that the foreshore was a good feeding or fattening ground for oysters. In 1773 800 acres of foreshore were leased for £600 for use as oyster layings to Messrs Lee, Harridge and King.

Conveyance of goods by sea was another industry that thrived in Southend. An admiralty return of 1564-5 shows that Prittlewell had 10 ships and owners and 16 seamen. Corn, timber, coal and other commodities would have been carried. In the 19th century the well-known family of Vandervord had a fleet of hoys and barges sailing to and from London.

The brewing industry developed in Southend during the 17th and 18th centuries, and in old Southend during the last century there was Lazarus' brewery. Southchurch Avenue was for a long time referred to as Brewery Road. This brewery was later bought by Lukers and transferred to the High Street. The brewery in High Street closed in 1933-4.

105. These fishermen's or oystermen's huts at the rear of Pleasant Row in Pleasant Road were erected by Outing in the 18th century before Pleasant Row itself was built. Each consisted of one room with a fireplace. They were destroyed in the 1960s.

106. The High Street, Southend, when it was still a pleasant tree-lined road. Luker's Brewery is on the right of the picture.

107. The works and house of Thomas Lindsell, coach builder, whose billhead is seen here, occupied the present site of the *Railway Hotel*, but were unfortunately destroyed by fire in 1872.

108. Luker's Brewery, High Street, Southend. It closed in 1934 and the site is now covered by the Presto supermarket and the Odeon cinema.

Windmills

There have been several windmills in the Southend area. The earliest recorded mill was built by Richard de Southchurch in 1294. It stood a little to the north of the junction of East Street and Sutton Road behind the old workhouse cottages that were sometimes known as Mill Hill Cottages and which were pulled down in 1960. A block of flats now occupies the site.

Another windmill was built in 1779 in East Street, but it was pulled down in about 1870. There was also one at Milton near to what is now Milton Road. It was probably in this mill that John de Holland, Duke of Exeter and uterine brother of King Richard II, was captured in 1400 while trying to flee the country after an unsuccessful plot against King Henry IV. This mill was advertised in 1800 by Mr. W. Jefferies, an auctioneer, as 'a capital Post Windmill driving two pairs of stones; in good repair. Good residence with oven and bakehouse attached, stables, coach house, piggeries and ten acres of arable and meadow land'.

109. Millfield House and the windmill which stood by it, West Street, Prittlewell (from a picture by Miss Norah Arber). This was a 'smock' mill and was pulled down about 1870.

110. Milton 'post' mill stood at the end of what is now Milton Road, on a corner site opposite Avenue Road
Baptist Church. The mill was pulled down in 1892 after being occupied in 1848 by Lazarus & Company and in
1874 by Thomas Arnold. It was still working as late as 1880.

Entertainment

The first recorded entertainment in Southend were plays which were performed at the *Grand* Hotel (now the *Royal*) and in a barn near the seafront. In 1803 Thomas Trotter, an actor manager from Worthing, secured a grant of land on what is now Easter Esplanade. The site was opposite and a little to the east of the *Minerva* and cost him £1,450 18s. It was described in 1824 as 'a small house at the eastern end of the town but neatly divided into boxes, pit and gallery'. Some of the leading actors and actresses played in Trotters *Theatre Royal*. Lady Hamilton, Nelson's famous mistress, is said to have been an enthusiastic patron in 1805 when she stayed at the *Royal* Hotel.

Trotter died in 1851. The year after his death the theatre was sold by his executors and in 1859, when owned by Mrs. G. Clarke, it was closed and converted into cottages or shops.

The Public Hall was built in Alexandra Street in 1872. It cost £3,000 to build. In 1886 it became the *Alexandra Theatre* and Public Hall, described in 1891 as 'chaste and elegant'. Mr. F. Marlow bought it in 1894, but it burnt down on 6 January 1895. In 1896 he rebuilt it at a cost of £25,000. Mr. Marlow went bankrupt, threw himself from the top of the theatre and was killed instantly. In the foundations under the present foyer of the ABC cinema are some remains of the old theatre; conventional hand signs still point the way to the pit and the stalls.

During the last years of the 19th century there was a portable theatre on the foreshore where plays such as the *Red Barn* and *East Lynn* were performed.

By 1908 entertainment was proceeding apace. Plans were passed for the *Hippodrome Variety Theatre* in Southchurch Road. At the first performance the flashlight of Mr. Shepherd, who was taking pictures of the audience, 'struck terror into the hearts of the ladies'. Also in 1908 the *Theatre de Luxe* cinema at Victoria Circus and the *Princes Picturedrome* in Tylers Avenue had opened. Previously, moving pictures of the Boer War had been projected at the *Criterion Palace of Varieties* on Marine Parade.

The bandstand, which was erected on the cliffs in 1909, replaced a wooden one which was was moved from the site to the Happy Valley. The well-known amusement centre, the Kursaal was opened in 1901 by Lord Claud Hamilton, Chairman of the Great Western Railway.

111.   The grounds and buildings of the Kursaal, seen here about 1905, covered 26 acres. The architect was Mr. C. Sherrin. By the time the property came up for auction in November 1903, £230,000 had been spent on the buildings and attractions; however, bidding rose no higher than £50,000 and it was withdrawn from the auction.

THEATRE, SOUTHEND.

BY DESIRE
AND UNDER THE IMMEDIATE PATRONAGE OF
THE STEWARDS OF THE BALL.

ON FRIDAY, SEPTEMBER 15, 1837,

Will be presented the much admired Petite Comedy, called

A HUSBAND AT SIGHT.

Ferdinand Louisberg....Mr. CHESTER.   Gustavus Gundershoff....Mr. MANN.
Paul Parchevetz....Mr. BROOKS.   Leonard....Mr. JONES.   Carl....Mr. J. CHESTER.
Baroness Louisberg....Mrs. CHESTER.
Augusta Polmshi....(diguised as Michael Von Inhapps)....Mrs LOVEGROVE.
Catherine....Mrs. NESSMITH.

Old English Gentleman (in character) Mr. BROOKS.
Tell me, have you seen a Toy? ....Mrs. LOVEGROVE.

After which the laughable Interlude of

Mr. & Mrs. WHITE

Major Pepper....Mr. BROOKS.   Frank Brown....Mr. MANN.
Peter White....Mr. J. CHESTER.
Widow White (with a Song) Mrs LOVEGROVE.
Mrs. White....(with a Duet and Dance)....Mrs. CHESTER.
Kitty Clover (with a Song) Mrs. NESSMITH.

Dolly the Dancing Dairy Maid....Mr. CHESTER.
Naval Hornpipe..(in character)..Mr. MANN.
I want Money ....Mr. J. CHESTER.

The whole to conclude with the laughable Farce, called

A Fashionable Husband.

Mr. Frederic Flighty (an erratic married Gentleman) Mr. CHESTER.
John (his Servant) Mr. BROOKS.
Mrs. Flighty   (an easy, confiding, unsuspecting Wife)   Mrs. CHESTER.
Mrs. Trictrac (a teasing tormenting young Widow) **Mrs. NESSMITH.**
Cornet Fitzherbert Fitzhenry (a regular killer and the Beau Ideal of a Cavalry Officer)
Mrs. NESSMITH.
Susan Twist (a well educated and accomplished Lady's Maid) Mrs. LOVEGROVE.

Doors open at Seven commence at half-past.   [*C. C. Noone, Printer, Rayleigh,*

112. Playbill for a programme presented at the Southend theatre in 1837. At this time Mr.
Chester was the stage manager and Mr. Mann the acting manager. The programmes were paid
for by private individuals and groups.

113.   The Empire Theatre was built in Alexandra Street in 1896 on the site of the Public Hall. It is seen here in 1907. In 1920 it was converted into the Rivoli Cinema, and in 1961 modernised and renamed the A.B.C.

114.   The Happy Valley on the cliffs, 1909. On the extreme right is Chigwin's Concert Party in performance. Many people seem to have gained a free view by standing, rather than by paying for a seat.

115. The first bandstand on the cliffs, about 1905. It was replaced by a new one and removed to the Happy Valley in 1909.

116. This bandstand, seen here in about 1910, was erected in 1909 by Messrs. Walter Macfarlane and Company at a cost of £750, and was opened by the Mayoress, Mrs. C. J. Ingram, on 29 May, when a programme of music was played by the band of the Royal Marines. Popularly known as the 'cakestand', it was demolished and replaced by a modern platform in 1956.

THE BANDSTAND, WESTCLIFF-ON-SEA.

117. Garon's Imperial Bioscope in the High Street, 1921. It cost £5,000 to build and opened in 1911. The auditorium seated 700 at first and 900 after enlargement. In the adjoining cafe, 300 persons could be accommodated. The cinema closed on 4 May 1963.

118. The demolition of the Gaumont Cinema in Southchurch Road in 1958: formerly the Hippodrome Music Hall, many famous names performed here, and lavish productions were staged.

Roads and Streets

One hundred years ago Southend High Street was a rural lane. When Dr. Deeping, father of the author Warwick Deeping, came to Southend in the last half of the 19th century there were very few buildings. There were two shops, owned by Mr. Brightwell and Mr. Chignall, a post office, the British School on the corner of Clarence Road, Mr. Weston's house and gardens (Weston Road is named after him) and Mr. Attridge's thatched cottage which stood on the corner of Cliff Town Road facing the London, Tilbury and Southend Railway Station. This last was described by the Doctor as looking 'like a magnificent shed'.

Further north was the *Middleton* Hotel and Luker's Middleton Brewery. There were no other buildings beyond this and the road continued, lined with hedges of hawthorn, sweet briar and blackberry bushes and many fine chestnut trees.

Whitegate, a 13-acre field which had an entrance opposite the station approach, was used for school sports and church fetes. The present Whitegate Road was laid out in 1881 and named Norfolk Street; the following year it was renamed Whitegate Road. The name was originally derived from a white-painted gate at what is now Victoria Circus and which was then White Gate Corner. The gate normally barred the public from the privately-owned High Street.

Southend station, the terminus of the railway line until 1884, was approached from Prittlewell by a field path if on foot, or if by vehicle by way of North Road or Sutton Road. The through road, Victoria Avenue, was opened in 1889.

Avenue Road was then a lane leading to Prittlewell; masses of primroses and violets grew there. What is now York Road was originally a lane leading to Mr. Heygate's meadow. It was known as Market Road and then became York Road, taking its name from the *Duke of York* Hotel. A small part of the hotel is now a shop on the south corner of the road at the junction with High Street.

Hamlet Court Road was also a winding country lane leading to Mr. Scudder's Hamlet Farm. Hamstel Road was then known as Stokers Lane.

On Marine Parade there were a number of greens, on which gipsies camped, between the houses and the shore. Three greens were eventually purchased by the Corporation: Fairhead's Green, on which fairs had been held, in 1884; Darlows Green and Fawley's Green in 1890 and 1901 respectively.

119. The High Street, Southend, on 9 June 1913. York Road can be seen on the right. Marks & Spencer now occupies the site of Smith's, the stationer and bookseller.

120. North Street, Prittlewell, seen here in 1878, is now Victoria Avenue. This picture was taken from the junction of West and East Streets. On the right is the *King's Arms*, and on the left the old *Spread Eagle*, not yet rebuilt. Many of these building have now vanished, but some, notably those with overhanging storeys, still remain.

121. The High Street in 1867. The thatched cottage stood at the junction of Cliff Town Road and High Street.

122. Looking southwards at the north end
of Hobleythick Lane, May 1924.

123. Prittlewell Hill early this century. Note the
rough surface of the road and absence of traffic.

124. This picture of Prittlewell Chase was taken at
the Hobleythick Lane end looking westwards, in 1924.

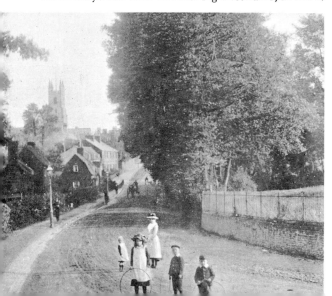

125. Victoria Circus and the *Hotel Victoria* (built *c.*1889), about 1925. From here buses went to Grays, London and villages around Southend. The open-top bus was going to Benfleet.

126. (*overleaf*) The High Street, Southend, looking north on 30 April 1914. On the right may be seen Byatt's Pork Butchery, noted for its sausages, and the *Hotel Victoria*. Trees grew on what is now the site of the Hammerston Development. Note the rough road surface and the tramlines.

Southend and the 1914-1918 War

Crowds waited outside the offices of the *Southend Standard* at midnight on 4 August 1914. They learnt that war had been declared on Germany because of her unprovoked attack on Belgium and there was loud cheering at the announcement.

Southend was a witness to the first air raid on this country. A German plane made its way over the estuary to Southend and flew up the river to Purfleet, then returned the way it had come without doing any damage. In May 1915 there were two Zeppelin raids in quick succession. In the early hours of 10 May many incendiary bombs were dropped. A special supplement of the *Southend Standard* stated that one woman was murdered. A message was attached to one bomb found in Rayleigh Avenue; 'You English we have come We'll come again. Kill or cure'. The bombs weighed about 50 lbs. and were very crude efforts. Feeling in the town ran high and a protest meeting was held. The windows and stock of several shops which had previously been occupied by Germans and Austrians were demolished. True to their promise the Germans came again on the night of 26 May. They dropped a large number of bombs starting many fires. A visitor to the town was killed near Chalkwell Park and two other women later died from their injuries.

On Sunday 12 May 1917 there was a terrible raid when the streets literally ran with blood. Twenty enemy Gotha planes dropped aerial torpedoes over the centre of the town and the eastern area. There were 15 minutes of terror; 35 people were killed and buildings were blown to pieces. Despite the war Southend was still very popular with day trippers and the crowds had stopped to watch the aircraft. Between Victoria Circus and the railway station were private houses, a cinema and rows of shops and coal offices. Fifteen people died in this area. Firemen had the dreadful task of clearing a path for people who were rushing to the station to return to London.

The *Southend Standard* showed in its windows on 11 November 1918 the news of the Kaiser's abdication and at 17 minutes to 11 that morning the gasworks' siren proclaimed that the armistice was to be signed. Southend streets were full of people and soldiers with decorated trucks paraded through the town.

127. Mrs. Whitwell, a well-known Salvationist, was asleep with her husband on 5 May 1915 when the German Zeppelins bombed the town. Mrs. Whitwell was killed; her husband, though severely burned, survived.

128. In mid-September 1914, the *Palace Hotel* became Queen Mary's Naval Hospital. Its first patients were 200 Belgian wounded; those shown above, however, are British soldiers. Queen Mary visited the hospital on 16 June 1915.

129. This photograph, taken on 24 August 1917, shows houses in Lovelace Lane which had been destroyed by German bombing twelve days previously.

130. Also photographed on 24 August, these houses in Guildford Road were also severely damaged by bombing.

131. West Street, Prittlewell, after the Zeppelin raid of 10 May 1915.

Shops

Before Southend itself existed Prittlewell or Rochford were the main centres of commerce. A fair was held at Prittlewell each November at which purchases could be made of commodities not available in the village. It was one of the great events of the year, but in 1665 it was not held because of the great risk of the spread of the plague. In 1872 it was discontinued as unnecessary and injurious to the residents. During the last few years of its existence it had operated mainly for the sale of toys and for amusement. It was held near the church and the churchyard was said to have been 'a common resort for debauchery'. However, with the growth of Southend shops became available on the sea front for its then aristocratic and fashionable visitors and the fair became obsolete.

The advertisements in the *Southend Standard* of 1871-3 give fascinating glances into the shops of that period. W. Lodder, jeweller of High Street, boasted of the patronage of H.R.H. Princess Louise and the Marquis of Lorne. H. Hassel, who was also a jeweller, silversmith and pawn broker as well as a tailor, sold men's black suits for £2 2s. (£2 10p) and gold rings for 4s. 6d. (22½p). J. J. Currie, ornamental hair manufacturer next to the Royal Nursery in High Street, disentangled and made up ladies' combings 'into any design or style whatsoever'. A. E. Hall, dyer and cleaner in Alexandra Street, would clean ladies' stays for 1s. (5p) a pair and the versatile Mr. K. J. Sykes, in 1875, had refreshment rooms four doors from the *London Tavern* and was also a fruiterer, confectioner and an entertainer with Punch and Judy, magic lantern etc. J. Echell of London attended at Mr. C. Ray's in Nelson Terrace. His advertisement has the strange wording 'Teeth new invention'.

There was obviously a very good milliner in Rochford during the last century as the author's grandmother, who lived in Prittlewell, went there to buy her hats.

32. All the best people bought their gardening requirements at Godward's in the High Street, near Weston Road, whose nursery was on the present site of the Alexandra Bowling Green. Princess Louise who had a large garden where the General Post Office now stands, patronised the shop.

QUALITY

CATERERS & CONT

OF PRIME
MUTTON & LAMB

Restaurant

H. GARON

133. (*overleaf*) Garon's shops by the railway bridge, High Street, on 7 February 1912. Harry Garon founded a grocery business in Prittlewell in 1882, and his son expanded the firm. In 1907 a company was floated and it was incorporated in 1908. By 1913 they were butchers, bakers, fishmongers, provision merchants, restauranteurs, as well as being the owners of a theatre and cinema.

134. (*above*) The *Golden Boot* in High Street stood next to the plot which subsequently became the entrance to Heygate Avenue.

135. (*right*) These three-wheeled milk carts came from the dairy of Mr. J. May on 9 Alexandra Street. The business was established in 1874.

136. In the 1880s Nelson Street was Southend's chief shopping centre, and was as busy as the High Street on a Saturday night. In 1953 the last of the old businesses (a greengrocey and poulterer which had been in the hands of one family for 70 years) closed down.

137.   Marks & Spencer opened in the High Street in 1914 as the Penny Bazaar—all goods cost just one penny. It is seen here about 1920.

138. An interior view of Marks & Spencer, about 1916.

139. (*right*) R. A. Jones & Sons Ltd was established in 1890 in the High Street. Mr. Jones introduced the novelty of giving free gifts to those who purchased rings worth more than 10s (50p). He was a great local benefactor, giving the priory site, the Jones Memorial Ground and, in 1921, the Victory Sports Ground to the town, the latter being a memorial to local sportsmen who died in the First World War. This photograph was taken in about 1914.

140. (*below*) The old post office, Southchurch, about 1908. It stood opposite the church and was demolished when the boulevard was built in 1913.

People, Places and Events

A number of notable people have been born in and lived in Southend and there have been many happy, sad and historic events.

A prominent figure of the last century was Daniel Scratton, lord of the manor of Prittlewell and one of the last of his family to live in the Priory. He was master of the South Essex Hunt and the hounds were kept at the Priory. It is said he did not always restrain his language in the hunting field but he was greatly esteemed. He died in 1902.

A very unusual series of events occurred when the Irish vicar of Prittlewell, Dr. F. Nolan, objected to the church bells being rung at times which were against his wishes. He grew exceedingly angry and entered the belfry carrying a carving knife to cut the bell ropes, and then employed the police to prevent the ringers entering the church. The ringers broke the Rectory windows and when they had gained entry to the church by mounting the roof and climbing into the belfry the vicar discharged pistols. So great was the dislike of Dr. Nolan that his effigy was burnt on 5 November.

141. This painting of Daniel Scratton, lord of the manor of Prittlewell, shows him on his brown hunter, Blackmore, with two couples of his hounds—Hebe, Solon, Comfort and Sentinel. It was painted by G. Pearce and cost 300 guineas. The painting was presented to Mrs. Scratton on 22 October 1897, and is now on loan to Prittlewell Priory Museum.

142. Thomas Dowsett, seen here in about 1893, was Southend's first mayor. Born about 1837,
he first worked as a crow scarer in the Prittlewell fields. Later he had a hairdressing establishment
and fancy goods shop on Marine Parade. He also developed estates in Southend, and built
Clifton Terrace, becoming one of the wealthiest men in the county. He was an active member of
Cliff Town church.

143. John Brightwell, mayor of Southend, in 1895. In 1873 he took over a drapery business next
to the *Royal Hotel*, and greatly expanded and improved it. It had become one of the best-known
and oldest stores in the town by the time it closed in the 1970s.

144. Kit Lester was the first town crier, and used to cry 'The news, church news, chapel news'. The *Southend Standard* reported in 1877 that 'Our Town Cryer has got his uniform coat, now he wants a cocked hat'. He died in Rochford House in 1901.

145. Dr. George Davidson Deeping, J.P., was a well-known figure in Southend for over 28 years. He was a member of the local **Board of Health**, and played an important part in stemming outbreaks of typhoid locally. He also played an important role in the establishment of Victoria Hospital. His son, Warwick Deeping, seen here as a boy, was a successful novelist. Born in Southend, three of his novels are set in the town: *The Dark House* (1941); *Mr. Slade* (1943); and *Mr. Gurney and Mr. Slade* (1944).

146. On the right of this picture of Southend High Street in 1905 is the *Royal Oyster Saloon*, formerly Prospect House, the home and surgery of Dr. Deeping, where his son Warwick was born in 1877. Dr. Deeping later moved to Royal Terrace.

147. Mr. and Mrs. Edward Kilworth sitting outside Southchurch Hall about 1850. The Kilworth family farmed at the Hall from the 1820s until 1892.

148. About 80 years ago this old couple used to take a live seal in a tank (its head is just visible in this picture) round the town. People used to throw pennies to them. When the seal died it was stuffed, and it could still be seen in recent years on the bar of the *Cornucopia* in Marine Parade.

149. Sophia Eliza Lindsell, who escaped from her father's burning coachbuilding works in Prittlewell, but lost the wedding dress and trousseau which she had been preparing for her marriage to A. J. Moss of Vange in the blaze.

150. The Crowstone was first erected about 1285, and marked the limit of the jurisdiction of the City of London. The stone was replaced in 1755 (seen in the picture left about 1818). Another larger replacement was installed in 1838 and the 1755 stone was erected in Priory Park. The Lord Mayor of London visited the Crowstone every seven years, and his name was incised upon it with the date. The Thames Conservancy then took over responsibility and in 1908 it was replaced in turn by the Port of London Commission.

151. Eastwood Lane (now called Kingsway), Westcliff, looking south and showing the old 18th-century Pest House which was an early form of isolation hospital. Situated away from the village, inhabitants with highly-contagious diseases were sent here to prevent the spread of infection. After 1840 the house was no longer used for this purpose, and became two tenements. It was demolished in 1914.

152. Victoria Hospital, Southend, was the result of a meeting between a group of local doctors in September 1886, who resolved to commemorate Queen Victoria's Jubilee. The foundation stone was laid in August 1887 by Lady Brooke, and the hospital opened the following year. It was replaced by Southend General Hospital in 1932, and the swimming pool now occupies the site.

153. Workhouse or Mill Hill Cottages, Sutton Road, Prittlewell, seen here before demolition in 1960. They were built in 1875 and housed paupers dependent on the workhouse. The inmates spun or carded wool, and were dressed in coarse dark grey clothing with a large 'P' on their collars. The building was sold to Daniel Scratton of the Priory in 1838, when Rochford Union Workhouse was built. The small brick building on the right was the parish lock-up or gaol.

154.   The reading of the charter of incorporation of Southend Borough to a crowd on Pier Hill, 19 September 1892. The Lord Mayor and Lady Mayoress of London are somewhere in the crowd.

155.   Jubilee celebrations in 1897. In the background is the Royal Library, Pier Hill, popular with the aristocratic and wealthy visitors of Southend's early days.

156. Mr. R. Whitehead (Liberal) was a successful candidate in the General Election of 1906, with a majority of over two thousand. He is seen here thanking his supporters.

157. In 1921 King George V visited Southend during Yachting Week, and his own yacht joined others in racing. In this picture the royal car is approaching what is now the site of the Hummerston Complex, Victoria Circus.

158. The Jolly Boys Concert Party, seen here in 1904, performed in their early years on the beach by Marine Parade, but later had a stage on the parade nearly opposite the Kursaal. The group was still in existence in 1927, with a successful formula of cross-talk and slapstick.

159. Building the *Hotel Metropole* in 1900. It was later renamed the *Palace Hotel*, and was a fashionable rendezvous in the years before the First World War.